FRANCHISING IN HONG KONG 2014

Legal and Business Considerations

KENDAL H. TYRE, JR., EXECUTIVE EDITOR
DIANA VILMENAY-HAMMOND, MANAGING EDITOR
PIERCE HAESUNG HAN, ASSISTANT EDITOR

LEXNOIR FOUNDATION

SECOND QUARTER 2014

LexNoir Foundation is the charitable, educational arm of LexNoir, an international network of lawyers connecting the African Diaspora.

This publication, *Franchising in Hong Kong 2014: Legal and Business Considerations*, contains excerpts from *Franchising in Asia 2014: Legal and Business Considerations*. Both works are published by LexNoir Foundation and reflect the points of view of the authors and editors as of the date of publication and do not necessarily represent the opinions, interpretations, or positions of the law firms or organizations with which they are affiliated, nor the opinions, interpretations or positions of LexNoir Foundation or LexNoir.

Nothing contained in this book is to be considered as the rendering of legal advice, either generally or in connection with any specific issues or case. Readers are responsible for obtaining advice from their own legal counsel or other professional. This book, any forms and agreements or other information herein are intended for educational and informational purposes only.

www.lexnoir.org

Table of Contents

Franchising in Hong Kong

David Allison
Bird & Bird

Page

Bibliography of International Franchise Resources

Kendal H. Tyre, Jr., Diana Vilmenay-Hammond, Pierce Haesung Han and Keri McWilliams
Nixon Peabody LLP

Acknowledgment

This book could not have been written without the hard work and dedication of each of the contributing authors and editors. Thank you.

We would like to acknowledge and extend our heartfelt gratitude to Maria Stallings of the Washington, D.C. office of Nixon Peabody LLP for her invaluable assistance in revising, proofing, and editing this publication.

About the Editors and Authors

Kendal H. Tyre, Jr. – Kendal is a partner in the Washington, D.C. office of Nixon Peabody LLP. He handles domestic and cross-border transactions, including mergers and acquisitions, joint ventures, strategic alliances, licensing, and franchise matters.

In his franchise and licensing practice, Kendal counsels domestic and international franchisors, franchisees, licensors, licensees and distributors regarding U.S. state and federal franchise laws as well as foreign franchise legislation in a variety of jurisdictions. Kendal drafts and provides advice with regard to franchise and license agreements, disclosure documents and area development agreements and has extensive experience drafting and negotiating a variety of other commercial agreements. His client base spans the United States and foreign countries, including South Africa, Kenya, and the United Kingdom.

Kendal is a frequent contributor to franchise publications and a frequent speaker at franchise programs held by the American Bar Association Forum on Franchising and the International Franchise Association.

Kendal is co-chair of the firm's Diversity Action Committee and its Africa Group. Kendal is also the executive director of LexNoir Foundation.

E-mail address: ktyre@nixonpeabody.com

Diana Vilmenay-Hammond – Diana is an attorney in the Washington, D.C. office of Nixon Peabody LLP. She is a member of the firm's Franchise & Distribution team.

In her franchise practice, Diana works with domestic and international franchisors on transactional and litigation matters. Specifically, she counsels franchisor clients regarding state and federal franchise laws, disclosure and registration obligations. Diana drafts and negotiates various commercial agreements, including international franchise and development agreements.

Diana has co-authored numerous articles on franchising and frequently co-hosted the Nixon Peabody franchise law webinar series. Topics have included:

- "Franchise Case Law Round-Up: Implications for Your Franchise;"
- "Social Media Part II: Best Practices in Protecting Your Brand in the New Media;" and
- "The Awuah Case: Bellwether or Outlier."

Diana received her J.D. from Howard University School of Law and her B.A. from Georgetown University. She is a member of the American Bar Association (Forum on Franchising).

E-mail address: dvilmenay@nixonpeabody.com

Pierce Haesung Han – Pierce is an associate in Nixon Peabody's Global Business & Transactions group. Pierce focuses his practice on three main areas, assisting clients with a variety of complex business transactions.

- Mergers & Acquisitions: Providing assistance to both public and private clients with various mergers and acquisitions, performing due diligence, drafting and negotiating transaction documents, and facilitating closing and post-closing mechanics.
- International Commercial Transactions: Drafting and negotiating a variety of commercial agreements, including international franchise and development agreements, license agreements, and purchase and sale agreements.

- Federal Securities Law Matters: Assisting public and private clients regarding federal securities laws and stock exchange rules relating to corporate governance and disclosure.

Pierce serves as the Secretary of the Asian Pacific Bar Association Educational Fund (an affiliate of the Asian Pacific American Bar Association of the Greater Washington, D.C. Area).

Pierce received his J.D. from Georgetown University Law Center and his B.A. from Case Western Reserve University. He is admitted to practice in the State of New York and the District of Columbia.

E-mail address: phan@nixonpeabody.com

Keri McWilliams – Keri is an associate in the Franchise & Distribution team of Nixon Peabody LLP. Keri works with clients on a number of franchising issues, including obtaining and maintaining franchise registrations in various states, responding to state inquiries regarding trade practices, ongoing compliance with state and federal regulations, and updating franchise disclosure documents. She also handles franchise sales counseling and franchise system issues.

Keri is a member of the American Bar Association's Forum on Franchising, and the Federal and Minnesota State bar associations. She is also a member of Minnesota Women Lawyers and the Minnesota Association of Black Lawyers, and a volunteer in the Volunteer Lawyers Network.

Keri received her J.D. from Georgetown University Law Center and her B.F.A. from Washington University. She is admitted to practice in the District of Columbia and Minnesota.

E-mail address: kmcwilliams@nixonpeabody.com

David Allison – David is Counsel within Bird & Bird's China IP team based in Hong Kong. With extensive experience in all major areas of intellectual property, including copyright, trademarks, patents, and registered designs, David has managed disputes dealing with infringement of trademarks, copyright as well as the misuse of confidential information and trade secrets. His particular areas of interest include contentious intellectual property disputes, the enforcement of intellectual property rights in both Hong Kong and mainland China, and the prosecution of trademark portfolios in Hong Kong and the greater China region. He also advises clients on non-contentious matters, particularly relating to personal data privacy. In addition to his litigation experience, David also has significant experience in the field of alternative dispute resolution. He is an accredited mediator and is a member of the Chartered Institute of Arbitrators. He also sits as a panelist for the Asian Domain Name Dispute Resolution Centre in Hong Kong.

Prior to joining Bird & Bird, David worked for both multinational and specialist law firms in Hong Kong and Australia in both IP and commercial litigation roles. He also acted as the Asia Pacific Regional IP Counsel for a major US MNC based in Shanghai.

David is qualified to practice law in the Supreme Court of Western Australia, the High Court of Australia and the High Court of Hong Kong.

E-mail address: david.allison@twobirds.com

About the Book

Franchising in Hong Kong 2014: Legal and Business Considerations contains excerpts from the larger work *Franchising in Asia 2014: Legal and Business Considerations*. Both books serve as practical, succinct, easy-to-use reference tools for lawyers, business people and academics to use in navigating the laws and business issues impacting franchise arrangements in Asia.

This book provides an overview of the franchise industry in Hong Kong and addresses the typical legal issues confronted when expanding a franchise system in Hong Kong. The larger work, *Franchising in Asia 2014: Legal and Business Considerations*, covers those laws governing franchising in several other Asian countries.

In both books, an author, who is a legal expert in the designated jurisdiction, addresses the basic questions that a franchise lawyer would need to know to competently represent a client in expanding their franchise system to that country.

Each country chapter organizes a discussion of that country's laws under various headings and in a uniform format. Topics were sent to each country's author in the form of a questionnaire, and each author drafted responses to the questions presented. A general overview relating to the political and economic history of the country at the beginning of each chapter provides an initial context for the regulatory framework.[1]

---

1 The source of information for these sections is the Central Intelligence Agency, https://www.cia.gov/library/publications/the-world-factbook/ (last visited July 10, 2014).

Apart from an overview of the legal framework for franchising, each book contains other articles and resources that should prove useful to those in the franchise industry.

The authors for each chapter are listed at the beginning of a chapter and their biographical information is listed in the previous section, *About the Editors and Authors*.

Readers should always consult with local counsel in the relevant jurisdiction instead of relying solely on the information contained in this book. The laws governing franchising are evolving and local counsel in Hong Kong are best positioned to provide timely, relevant advice applying the current law to the particular facts of a case.

Franchising in Hong Kong

David Allison
Bird & Bird
Hong Kong, China

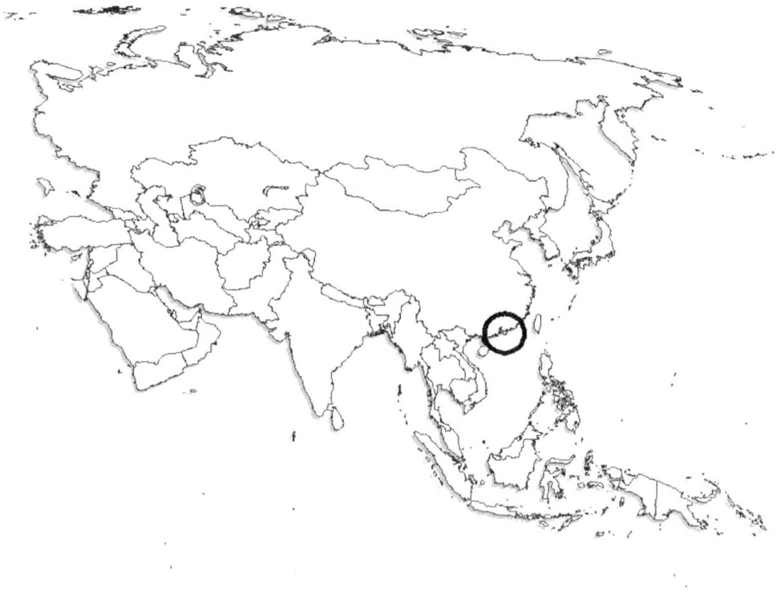

I. Introduction

A. Historical Background of the Country

Pursuant to an agreement signed by China and the United Kingdom on December 19, 1984, Hong Kong became the Hong Kong Special Administrative Region (SAR) of the People's Republic of China on July 1, 1997. In this agreement, China promised that, under its "one country, two systems" formula, China's socialist economic system would not be imposed on Hong Kong and that Hong Kong would enjoy a "high degree of autonomy" in all matters except foreign and defense affairs for the subsequent 50 years.

B. Economy of the Country

Hong Kong has a free market economy, highly dependent on international trade and finance - the value of goods and services trade, including the sizable share of re-exports, is about four times GDP. Hong Kong has no tariffs on imported goods, and it levies excise duties on only four commodities, whether imported or produced locally: hard alcohol, tobacco, hydrocarbon oil, and methyl alcohol. There are no quotas or dumping laws. Hong Kong's open economy left it exposed to the global economic slowdown that began in 2008. Although increasing integration with China, through trade, tourism, and financial links, helped it to make an initial recovery more quickly than many observers anticipated, its continued reliance on foreign trade and investment leaves it vulnerable to renewed global financial market volatility or a slowdown in the global economy.

The mainland has long been Hong Kong's largest trading partner, accounting for about half of Hong Kong's total trade by value. Hong Kong's natural resources are limited, and food and raw materials must be imported. As a result of China's easing of travel restrictions, the number of mainland tourists to the territory has surged from 4.5 million in 2001 to 34.9 million in 2012, outnumbering visitors from all other countries combined.

Hong Kong has also established itself as the premier stock market for Chinese firms seeking to list abroad. In 2012 mainland Chinese companies constituted about 46.6% of the firms listed on the Hong Kong Stock Exchange and accounted for about 57.4% of the Exchange's market capitalization. During the past decade, as Hong Kong's manufacturing industry moved to the mainland, its service industry has grown rapidly. Credit expansion and tight housing supply conditions have caused Hong Kong property prices to rise rapidly; consumer prices increased by more than 4% in 2013. Lower and middle income segments of the population are increasingly unable to afford adequate housing.

Hong Kong continues to link its currency closely to the US dollar, maintaining an arrangement established in 1983. In 2013, Hong Kong and China signed new agreements under the Closer Economic Partnership Agreement, adopted in 2003 to forge closer ties between Hong Kong and the mainland. The new measures, effective from January 2014, cover services and trade facilitation, and will improve access to the mainland's service sector for Hong Kong-based companies.

C. Franchise Legal Overview

Although a part of the People's Republic of China, Hong Kong has its own distinct legal system which has its base in English common law. It has no franchise-specific law.

II. Regulatory Requirements

A. Pre-Sale Disclosure

Please describe any pre-sale franchise disclosure or similar requirements that may apply to franchise transactions.

Hong Kong has no specific legislation or set of regulations that deal with franchising. Accordingly, the ordinary principles of contract and the common law will apply to franchises in Hong Kong.[2]

B. Governmental Approvals, Registrations, Filing Requirements

Please describe any necessary government approvals, registrations, or filing requirements that may apply to franchise transactions.

There are no government approvals, registrations or filing requirements that apply to franchise transactions in Hong Kong.

---

2 *Editor's Note:* Although there are no disclosure requirements mandated under the laws of Hong Kong, the Hong Kong Franchise Association ("HKFA") has established a Code of Ethics, which provides that a franchisor should issue to the prospective franchisee full and accurate written disclosure of all information material to the franchise relationship within a reasonable time prior to the execution of the agreement. The Hong Kong General Chamber of Commerce established HKFA to monitor and promote the development of franchising. Membership in HKFA is voluntary.

C. Limits on Fees and Typical Term of Franchise Agreement

Please describe any limits upon the nature and extent of fees and the term of a typical franchise agreement.

No limit has been prescribed on the nature and rate of the franchise fees and the term of a typical franchise agreement.

III. Currency

If all payments under a franchise agreement must be made in immediately available U.S. Dollars, please advise as to any restrictions, reporting requirements, or regulations concerning the exchange, repatriation or remittance of U.S. Dollars.

Hong Kong maintains no restrictions in terms of currency. Parties are free to use whichever currency they wish in relation to their franchise and there are no exchange controls or restrictions in place. It is common to find agreements in Hong Kong being denominated in Hong Kong Dollars, US dollars or sometimes Chinese renminbi.

IV. Taxes, Tariffs and Duties

Please do not provide any in-depth comments on tax structuring. However, please provide your general comments on the typical amount of withholding tax that would apply and whether a "gross-up" provision contained in a franchise agreement would be enforceable in your country.

Hong Kong maintains a relatively straightforward tax system operating under the *Inland Revenue Ordinance* (Cap. 112). Key features include a simple flat tax rate based on all profits arising in or derived from Hong Kong. Because only Hong Kong based profits are taxed, companies will not be subject to tax on income they receive from sources outside Hong Kong. There are in any event a number of bi-lateral double tax treaties in place with various foreign jurisdictions.[3]

While Hong Kong does not impose withholding tax on dividends or interest, withholding tax may be imposed in relation to royalty payments made to a non-resident in respect of use of intellectual property.

V. Trademarks

Please advise us as to whether there are any special requirements for granting a valid trademark license, including the use of a registered user agreement or a short trademark license agreement and any required filing of such an agreement with the trademark authorities.

Trademarks in Hong Kong are governed by the *Trade Marks Ordinance* (Cap. 559) ("Ordinance"). Under the Ordinance, a trademark license may be either "general" or "limited". The license must be in writing and must be duly executed by the licensor either by signature or by affixing the corporate seal.

---

3 *Editor's Note:* The list of countries and territories that have double taxation treaties with Hong Kong are provided on the following site, see http://www.ird.gov.hk/eng/tax/dta_inc.htm (last visited July 10, 2014).

4 *Editor's Note:* The IPD maintains a database of trademarks, patents and registered designs that enables individuals to search for intellectual property currently registered with the IPD. See http://ipsearch.ipd.gov.hk/index.html (last visited July 10, 2014).

A license agreement is a registrable transaction in Hong Kong and must be registered with the Hong Kong Intellectual Property Department ("IPD").[4] Failure to do so will deprive the licensee with rights under the Ordinance, including rights in relation to infringement and taking action to enforce the trademark.

Recordal of the license is made by filing the relevant forms with the IPD and paying the recordal fee (currently HK$800 – approximately US$100). It is not necessary to produce a copy of the license when filing for recordal of the license unless specifically requested by the IPD.

Recordal of a license with the IPD is essentially a procedural matter and recordal is almost always granted unless the application is deficient in terms of basic information required on the application form or if the application has not been signed by the licensor.

VI. Restrictions on Transfer

Please advise as to whether there are any restrictions (1) on a franchisor to restrict transfers by a master franchisee, any interest in a master franchisee, or the assets of the master franchisee or (2) the ability of a master franchisee to control and/or restrict transfers of a subfranchisee's rights under a master franchise agreement, an interest in the subfranchisee, or the assets of the subfranchisee.

There are no specific restrictions on transfer in Hong Kong. These are matters for the parties to agree between themselves.

VII. Termination

Please advise us as to any laws relating to termination in your country, such as agency laws, required indemnity provisions, notice or "good cause" requirements, or other laws affecting termination of a franchise agreement. Please describe.

There are no special restrictions on termination of a Franchise agreement in Hong Kong. Ordinary common law principles of contract will apply.

VIII. Governing Law, Jurisdiction and Dispute Resolution

A. Choice of Law of Foreign Jurisdiction

Please confirm whether the choice of law of a foreign jurisdiction would likely to be upheld under the law of the country, except for certain matters such as trademarks, bankruptcy and competition matters, which we assume would be governed by the law in your country.

Parties are generally free to choose the laws of a foreign jurisdiction to apply when interpreting their franchise agreement or for the purpose of dispute resolution. The courts in Hong Kong will generally respect party choice regarding jurisdiction subject only to the usual common law rules relating to conflict of laws.

B. International Arbitration Dispute Resolution

Please confirm that a court in your country would honor an election of international arbitration dispute resolution, and therefore refuse to hear any disputes arising under a franchise agreement.

Hong Kong can be described as a very pro-international arbitration jurisdiction. Arbitration matters are regulated by the *Arbitration Ordinance* (Cap. 609) which draws heavily upon the UNCITRAL Model Law. With very few exceptions, Hong Kong courts would honor parties election of international arbitration for dispute resolution.

Hong Kong is a signatory to the *Convention on the Recognition and Enforcement of Foreign Arbitral Awards* (the "New York Convention").[5]

IX. Non-Competitive Provisions

If the franchise agreement prohibits the franchisee from engaging in certain competitive activities during the term of the agreement, and for a 12-month period after the termination or expiration of the agreement, please comment on the enforceability of non-competition covenants in your country.

As there is no specific legislation dealing with franchising in Hong Kong, parties are at liberty to agree on their own non-competition covenants.

There are, however, common law restrictions that will apply to any non-competition provisions that parties may wish to insert in employees' contracts of employment. It is broad public policy that an employee should be entitled to work for whomever they wish after termination of employment. This is subject only to an employer's right to protect identifiable business interests by restricting the ability of an employee to work for direct competitors upon termination. In general, the post-termination restriction should not be termed as a "non-compete" provision *per se* but rather it should be addressed at a specific, identifiable

---

5 *Editor's Note:* Arbitral awards made in Hong Kong are also enforceable in mainland China under the *Arrangement Concerning Mutual Enforcement of Arbitral Awards* which is between mainland China and Hong Kong.

threat and should be no wider than is reasonably necessary, both in terms of time and geography, to protect the employer's legitimate business interest.

Outside the employment sphere, Hong Kong does not currently have in force any specific competition or anti-trust legislation. However, the recently enacted *Competition Ordinance* (Cap. 619) ("Competition Ordinance") may have an impact in the future for franchises whose conduct has the object or effect of restricting competition in Hong Kong either through anti-competitive agreements between undertakings or through the abuse of substantial market power. The Competition Ordinance has not yet come into effect in Hong Kong.

X. Language Requirements

Does the law in your country require that a franchise agreement be translated into the local language in order to be enforceable between the parties?

There is no requirement that franchise agreements be translated into the local language in Hong Kong and a franchise agreement may be concluded in any language.

It should be noted however, that Hong Kong has two official languages, Chinese and English, for the purposes of any communications with the Government or court proceedings (see *Official Languages Ordinance* Cap. 5). Accordingly, in practice most franchise agreements in Hong Kong are drawn up in either English or Chinese.

XI. Other Significant Matters

Please advise as to whether there are any significant matters not addressed above of which a franchisor should be aware in connection with its entering into a franchise agreement in your country.

As previously noted, the key body dealing with franchising in Hong Kong is the Hong Kong Franchising Association – see www.franchise.org.hk. This is a body organized within the Hong Kong General Chamber of Commerce.[6]

---

[6] *Editor's Note:* Although there is no official record of the total number of franchise operators in Hong Kong, records of the Hong Kong Franchising Association indicate that there were about 55 franchise operators in 1992. The number of franchise operators grew to 95 in 1997, and ultimately reached 124 in 1999. At present, there are approximately 75 franchise operators in Hong Kong. Of these franchise operators, 56% are local franchises. 42.7% of the franchises in Hong Kong are in catering business, 37.3% in services and 20% in retailing.

Bibliography of International Franchise Resources

Kendal H. Tyre, Jr., Diana Vilmenay-Hammond, Pierce Haesung Han and Keri McWilliams
Nixon Peabody LLP
Washington, D.C.

I. General International Resources

Mark Abell, Gary R. Duvall, and Andrea Oricchio Kirsh, *International Franchise Legislation* B1, ABA FORUM ON FRANCHISING (1996)

Kathleen C. Anderson and Anthony M. Stiegler, *Put Muscle in Your Marks: Enforcing Intellectual Property Rights* W14, ABA FORUM ON FRANCHISING (1995)

Richard M. Asbill and Jane W. LaFranchi, *International Franchise Sales Laws—A Survey* W7, ABA FORUM ON FRANCHISING (2005)

Jeffery A. Brimer, Alison C. McElroy, and John Pratt, *Going International: What Additional Restraints Will You Face?* W4, ABA FORUM ON FRANCHISING (2011)

Michael G. Brennan, Alexander Konigsberg, and Philip F. Zeidman, *Globetrotting: A Workshop on International Franchising* 10/W8, ABA FORUM ON FRANCHISING (1994)

Michael G. Brennan, Alexander Konigsberg, and Philip F. Zeidman, *Globetrotting: Strategies for Launching U.S.*

Franchisors Abroad 2/P2, ABA FORUM ON FRANCHISING (1994)

Christopher P. Bussert and Jennifer Dolman, *Regaining Your Trademark After Abandonment or Misappropriation* W7, ABA FORUM ON FRANCHISING (2011)

Ronald T. Coleman and Linda K. Stevens, *Trade Secrets and Confidential Information: Rights and Remedies* W2, ABA FORUM ON FRANCHISING (2000)

Finola Cunningham, *Commerce Department Helps Franchisors Go Global*, in FRANCHISING WORLD 63 (Dec. 2005)

Michael R. Daigle and Alex S. Konigsberg, *Meeting Off-Shore Disclosure and Contract Requirements* F/W13, ABA FORUM ON FRANCHISING (1992)

Jennifer Dolman, Robert A. Lauer, and Lawrence M. Weinberg, Structuring International Master Franchise Relationships for Success and Responding When Things Go Awry W22, ABA FORUM ON FRANCHISING (2007)

Gary R. Duvall, Paul Jones, and Jane LaFranchi, *Planning for the International Enforcement of Franchise Agreements* W6, ABA FORUM ON FRANCHISING (1999)

William Edwards, International Expansion: Do Opportunities Outweigh Challenges? in FRANCHISING WORLD (February 2008)

George J. Eydt and Stuart Hershman, *Bringing a Foreign Franchise System to the United States* W9, ABA FORUM ON FRANCHISING (2009)

William A. Finkelstein and Louis T. Pirkey, *International Trademarks* W15, ABA FORUM ON FRANCHISING (1991)

William A. Finkelstein, Protecting Trademarks Internationally: Current Strategies and Developments B3, ABA FORUM ON FRANCHISING (1996)

Stephen Giles, Lou H. Jones, and Lawrence Weinberg, *Negotiating and Documenting Complex International Franchise Agreements* W21, ABA FORUM ON FRANCHISING (2006)

Steven M. Goldman, Stephen Giles, Marc Israel, and Stanley Wong, *Competition Round Up from Around the World* LB2, ABA FORUM ON FRANCHISING (2004)

David C. Gryce and E. Lynn Perry, *Trademarks and Copyrights in the International Arena* 6/W4, ABA FORUM ON FRANCHISING (1993)

Kenneth S. Kaplan, Andrew P. Loewinger, and Penelope J. Ward, *System Standards in International Franchising* W14, ABA FORUM ON FRANCHISING (2005)

Edward Levitt and Jorge Mondragon, A Survey of International Legal Traps and How to Avoid Them—Beyond the Franchise Laws W20, ABA FORUM ON FRANCHISING (2007)

Ned Levitt, Kendal H. Tyre, and Penny Ward, *The Impossible Dream: Controlling Your International Franchise System* W4, ABA FORUM ON FRANCHISING (2010)

Michael K. Lindsey and Andrew P. Loewinger, *International (Non-U.S.) Franchise Disclosure Requirements* W9, ABA FORUM ON FRANCHISING (2002)

Andrew P. Loewinger and John Pratt, *Recent Changes and Trends in International Franchise Laws* W4, ABA FORUM ON FRANCHISING (2008)

Andrew P. Loewinger and Thomas M. Pitegoff, Avoiding the Long Arm of the Law in International Franchising: Issues and Approaches W8, ABA FORUM ON FRANCHISING (1995)

Craig J. Madson and Katherine C. Spelman, *Similarity and Confusion in the Intellectual Property Arena* W11, ABA FORUM ON FRANCHISING (1997)

Christopher A. Nowak, John Pratt, and Carl E. Zwisler, *Franchising Internationally with Countries with Opaque Legal Systems* W20, ABA FORUM ON FRANCHISING (2006)

E. Lynn Perry and John L. Sullivan Jr., *Trademark Compliance and Enforcement Techniques* E/W12, ABA FORUM ON FRANCHISING (1992)

Marcel Portmann, *Franchising Sector Proves Global Reach*, in FRANCHISING WORLD (January 2007)

John Pratt and Luiz Henrique O. do Amaral, Civil Law for Common Law Practitioners (or How to Draft an Agreement for Use Overseas) W4, ABA FORUM ON FRANCHISING (2002)

Kirk W. Reilly, Robert F. Salkowski and Geoffrey B. Shaw, *Determining the Rules of Engagement in Litigation Here and Abroad* W5, ABA FORUM ON FRANCHISING (2008)

Catherine Riesterer and Frank Zaid, *Basics of International Franchising* L/B2, ABA FORUM ON FRANCHISING (1997)

W. Andrew Scott and Christopher N. Wormald, *Stranger in a Strange Land: Contrasting Franchising in International Expansion* W2, ABA FORUM ON FRANCHISING (2003)

Donald Smith and Erik Wulff, *International Franchising: The Unraveling of an International Franchise Relationship* 15/W13, ABA FORUM ON FRANCHISING (1993)

Frank Zaid, Pamela Mills, and Michael Santa Maria, *Essential Issues in International Franchising* LB/1, ABA FORUM ON FRANCHISING (2001)

II. Asian Resources

Stephen Giles, Andrew P. Loewinger, and Sherin Sakr, *Go East Young Franchisor: Franchising in Asia-Pacific Other Than China and India* W21, ABA FORUM ON FRANCHISING (2011)

Stephen Giles, *Franchising in Asia-Pacific Region, Who's Who Legal*: FRANCHISE 2012 (2012)

A. China

Ren Yanling, *Changes to Chinese Franchise Law: An improved Balance Between the Interests of Franchisors and Franchisees*, in INT'L JOURNAL OF FRANCHISING LAW 3 (2012)

China: New Franchsing Law, in Int'l Journal of FRANCHISING LAW 2 (2005)

Ella S.K. Cheong, *China*, in INTERNATIONAL FRANCHISING CHN/1 (Dennis Campbell gen. ed. 2011)

Yu Qin and Richard L. Wageman, *China*, in INTERNATIONAL FRANCHISE SALES LAWS China-1 (Andrew P. Loewinger and Michael K. Lindsey eds. 2010)

Mark Abell, Daniela C. Brito, and Paul D. Jones, *Franchising in the BRIC Markets (Brazil, Russia, India, and China)* W18, ABA FORUM ON FRANCHISING (2008)

B. Hong Kong

Andrea S.Y. Fong, *Hong Kong*, in INTERNATIONAL FRANCHISING HK/1 (Dennis Campbell gen. ed. 2011)

C. India

Preeti Mehta, *India—Termination of Master Franchise Agreements and the Consequences*, in INT'L JOURNAL OF FRANCHISING LAW 3 (2007)

Yoginder Pal, *Franchising in India*, FRANCHISING WORLD (October 2006)

Mark Abell, Daniela C. Brito and Paul D. Jones, *Franchising in the BRIC Markets (Brazil, Russia, India, and China)* W18, ABA FORUM ON FRANCHISING (2008)

D. Indonesia

Sigit Ardianto and Rivan F. Ramadhan, *Indonesia*, in INTERNATIONAL FRANCHISING INA/1 (Dennis Campbell gen. ed. 2011)

Rick Beckman and Ferry P. Madian, *Indonesia*, in INTERNATIONAL FRANCHISE SALES LAWS Indonesia-1 (Andrew P. Loewinger and Michael K. Lindsey eds. 2010)

Kendal H. Tyre, Jr. & Pierce Haesung Han, *The Ministry of Trade of Indonesia Limits Growth of Food and Beverage*

Franchises, Nixon Peabody LLP: Franchise Alert (February 2013)

E. Japan

Takenari Shimizu, *Japan*, in International Franchising JAP/1 (Dennis Campbell gen. ed. 2011)

Souichirou Kozuka and Takashi Kanai, *Japan*, in International Franchise Sales Laws Japan-1 (Andrew P. Loewinger and Michael K. Lindsey eds. 2010)

F. Malaysia

Leela Baskaran, *Malaysia*, in International Franchising MAY/1 (Dennis Campbell gen. ed. 2011)

Mohd Bustaman Hj Abdullah and Wong Sai Fong, *Malaysia*, in International Franchise Sales Laws Malaysia-1 (Andrew P. Loewinger and Michael K. Lindsey eds. 2010)

Kendal H. Tyre, Jr. & Pierce Haesung Han, *Malaysian Government Actively Promotes Growth in Franchise Sector*, Nixon Peabody LLP: Franchise Alert (October 2013)

Kendal H. Tyre, Jr. & Pierce Haesung Han, *Tapping Into Malaysia's Aggressive Franchising Goals*, Portfolio Media, Inc.: Law360 (November 2013)

G. Singapore

Daniel Lim, Bernard Lui, Michele The, and Vanessa Chew, *Singapore*, in International Franchising SIN/1 (Dennis Campbell gen. ed. 2011)

H. South Korea

Brendon Carr and Jae-Hoon Kim, *South Korea*, in INTERNATIONAL FRANCHISE SALES LAWS South Korea-1 (Andrew P. Loewinger and Michael K. Lindsey eds. 2010)

Kendal H. Tyre, Jr. & Pierce Haesung Han, *South Korea adopts major amendments to the Fair Transactions in Franchise Business Act*, NIXON PEABODY LLP: FRANCHISE LAW ALERT (January 2014)

I. Taiwan

Wellington Liu and David Lu, *Taiwan*, in INTERNATIONAL FRANCHISE SALES LAWS Taiwan-1 (Andrew P. Loewinger and Michael K. Lindsey eds. 2010)

J. Thailand

Alan Adcock and Sriwan Puapondh, *Thailand*, in INTERNATIONAL FRANCHISING THA/1 (Dennis Campbell gen. ed. 2011)

K. Vietnam

Mai Minh Hang and Nguyen Anh Tran, *Vietnam*, in INTERNATIONAL FRANCHISE SALES LAWS Vietnam-1 (Andrew P. Loewinger and Michael K. Lindsey eds. 2010)

14932774.2

Printed in Dunstable, United Kingdom

91343664R00020